ALSO BY MELISSA FITE JOHNSON

Green
A Crooked Door Cut into the Sky (chapbook)
Ghost Sign (collaboration)
While the Kettle's On

MIDLIFE ABECEDARIAN

Melissa Fite Johnson

Riot in Your Throat
publishing fierce, feminist poetry

Johnson, Melissa Fite.
1st edition.
ISBN: 979-8-9889898-1-3

Cover Art: Sean Benesh (unsplash.com)
Cover Design: Jai Johnson
Book Design: Shanna Compton
Author Photo: Meryl Carver-Allmond

Riot in Your Throat
Arlington, VA
www.riotinyourthroat.com

For Generation Catalano

CONTENTS

PART THREE

I am telling you, we had a time. Didn't we? Didn't we have a time?
    —Rayanne Graff, *My So-Called Life*

Look! We have all
turned into
ourselves.
    —Linda Pastan, "25th High School Reunion"

WALKING SONNET

The wind insists. My hand holds down my hat,
our littlest dog's fur ruffled like waves.
Yet the men hammer the not-yet apartment's roof.
One man kneels right on the edge.
I imagine shingles gusting in all directions
like graduation caps, like confetti. I imagine him
hypnotized and falling. I don't want to
watch him die, or anyone, though his death
would make a more memorable poem.
Under these conditions, I'm fine with boring poems:
My husband asks what kind of tea I'd like and makes it.
My mom finally understands why dogs not kids.
The man braces himself, resumes his work.
We walk home, make tea, nap all afternoon.

We walk home, make tea, nap all weekend.
On Monday, I ask students to be present. They hold
votives in their hands, a tiny midnight mass.
Light echoes their cast-down faces. I'm pouring
my heart out. I'm tired. This relentless desire
to suck life's marrow born from *Dead Poets Society*,
not actually Thoreau, my view all table climbing
to sneer down on the conquered world,
checkmark checkmark checkmark. My exhaustion
proof of day-seizing. My disappointment when
they're in a world untethered from my room.
When a student connects eyes with mine,
speaks in a butterfly voice, fluttery and breathless
revelation, I know better than to barge in.

I know better than to expect revelation
at the grocery store. Become small talk,
become small. Parents shake their heads, distracted,
double-checking lists. *Not now, baby.*
A man squints at his phone. A young couple argues.
A mother's child, soundless slow motion.
She buys him a candy bar. She shuffles to the van.
We forget, absently opening doors, selecting
the malleable peas, ice cream brick, where
we're all headed. Not heaven. Not hell.
Not into a five-pound baby. Into a box.
Into the ground. Shrugging off our skin
and becoming what we were always going to be.
Death, so ordinary it stars every poem. It's boring.

Love, so ordinary it stars every song. It's boring,
how every couple in love thinks they invented it.
Maybe a miracle should be more miraculous,
more spaceship, more pushing up from the wheelchair
to walk, more talking the shooter out of it.
We miracle every sunset, miracle the moon. Still—
Joni Mitchell wrote *River* a decade before my birth.
Nothing to do with me. But in 1988, I was seven
and the song accompanied Kevin Arnold's lonely walk
on Christmas. Green letter jacket, tartan scarf,
he dressed like the trees she sang about.
Hands in his pockets, wishing Winnie Cooper
loved him back. I wasn't too young
to understand—it would take a miracle.

It would take a miracle to understand
if birds have dreams, if any bird is famous,
if birds have to remind themselves
flying is what matters, no show-off loop-de-loops,
no need to be the one framed in the binoculars' glass.
Open the window, birds call and answer.
Beyond the window, the wetlands where we walk
our dogs. Some days I force the view—
blue sky and blue marsh and blue birds.
But it's beautiful even in winter, better the waterfowl
than the hawk. We follow the snow, no sense
of time—we are 29, we are nine, we are 80
lying down to die. A memory before it happens,
it is the tunnel and it is the light.

The light at the end of the tunnel:
the dog on the other side. When our dog
gnaws the fence, I shout his name.
Sometimes this is enough to stop his destruction.
Blood on the splintered post, blood at his mouth.
What compels our dog to risk injury?
He wants what we all want: to be heard.
He can bark for hours without us knowing why.
After his strokes, my father mouthed his orders
at restaurants while servers cast their eyes
longingly at someone else's table. In a decade,
our dog will loaf the lawn and we'll ache
for his run. In twenty years, he'll be
a picture on the wall, and in sixty so will we.

In sixty years we'll be a picture on the wall.
How is this possible? We once thought
forty sounded old, couldn't imagine ourselves
saying *Not in this household, young lady!*
Or young man. Who knew who our kids would be?
Whose gold on our fingers? The future flung
before us, a piñata we swiped at, blindfolded.
At twenty, a fortuneteller stopped me
on a San Francisco street: tall dark handsome,
the usual assurances, but the future
she sold me came true. Half my life ago.
At eighty I'll call midlife youth, scold myself for
inspecting sunspots and lines. Be present:
the wind insists. My hand holds down my hat.

PART ONE

WHEN WE WERE YOUNG, WE OWNED THE SKY

Go back to when we had no clue what our majors would be,
when we wondered future husbands. In art class,
we drew antlers our teacher had stolen from
her ex-husband's wall. It was her wall then, too.
During fire drills, we charted clouds. Isn't it beautiful,
for the whole sky to feel like yours? We could be anyone
except ourselves. In college we shopped McDonald's
for ketchup and salt, sang ourselves hoarse in the car.
At night we climbed downtown ladders, mittens and coats,
played Truth, so much better than Dare. I slipped
and said I loved Nick, when I knew Erin also loved Nick.
We chalked it up to great minds and buzzed more beer,
lingered more cigarettes. When rain swelled the air,
we opened our arms, waited to be raptured out of this town.

SPEECHLESS

First date, bowling alley. Poor choice, no chance to talk,
one of us always taking a turn. When he bowled, his hip curved,
same stance as when he played trumpet, school band where we met.
After two games, still silent, we held hands in our center lane,
the eye, movement all around us, bowlers, spinning orbs.
Disco night, music our parents might have danced to. So nervous,
I couldn't talk, five weeks of me clearing my throat,
then changing my mind. What to say? I love you, why me,
why not Jessica or Erin, I've only kissed one other boy
who clearly taught me nothing. Our nightly phone call, daily cafeteria,
three more dates: silence. Parking lot. He started the truck,
February cold, fogged his cupped hands, turned to me. I accepted
his kiss, returned to it years later, astral projection,
in other relationships, when having sex and not wanting to, when
pinned to a mattress on a living room floor, when
being held by my throat in a doorway. He started the truck.
His hand on my hair. Proof nothing bad would happen in my life.

A MAN I DIDN'T SLEEP WITH ASKED WHAT WORD DEFINED ME

Beginning, I said. He began dissecting my choice. No –ing words,
no developing or growing—who are you now, not who are you
beginning to be? I began stammering. I didn't like not being believed,
I knew that, even if I didn't know anything else about myself.
I'd begun the day not knowing him. I began it at the coffee shop,
heartbroken and eating a muffin, Mazzy Star accompanying
the barista's sweeping, a lonely dance that took her to each corner
of the room and nowhere else. He began it asking a stranger to join him.
I did. We began talking, or I began talking and he began correcting.
Subtly, but I noticed. I just didn't like myself enough to stop him.
Lunch. A walk. Dinner. He looked a little like Ryan Phillipe
if Ryan Phillipe had a mohawk. Somehow, we ended up in his apartment.
In his bed. We began kissing, but that's all. Summer, but I wore
long sleeves, jeans, sneakers. Armor. Already weary at twenty.
He asked to take a picture of me naked. I said no. I found that flattering,
but I don't, looking back. He called the next day, the next.
I let the phone ring. I was beginning. He didn't know me at all.

BEFORE SUNRISE ON THE VCR

I'd never felt this before, pulse and breath. Oh, I wanted him.
We'd steal a bottle of red from the bar, sleep in the park. I longed for
the 90s, some wistful before, though it *was* the 90s.

Ode to his leather jacket and goatee.
Ode to her jumper and baby tee. Before the first day of school,
I laid out an approximation of her outfit on my bed—

I wanted to be her, before my father died, before
my brother moved to Rhode Island. Before my mother and I
had weekly therapy, before my mother's new husband said

the best thing about me was my tits. Before boyfriends
took what they wanted while I hovered outside
my body, a basin brimming with others' needs.

My husband asked before even holding my hand.
Our first date not in Vienna but at our hometown Mall Deli.
I don't give my words to street poets anymore. I'll write the poems.

TRUTH

is fuzzy   the frayed rope I climbed in 6th grade gym
strong enough to hold   but I imagined a fall
every time   I could hear laughter   They laughed
because I went to Hardee's to watch TV

The truth is we couldn't afford cable
The truth is I had to watch *Are You Afraid of the Dark*

Thirty years later someone tells me they like my sweater
and I say   *Thanks! It cost a dollar!*

Truth looms like the giant   inflatable beach ball
we sat in a circle and kicked   the parachute
we all held a piece of in our hands

Truth holds suspended   in the moments
it hesitates before landing

Thirty years later I'm comfortable with silence
I no longer say   *So here we are*
     for no reason

Truth is uniform
thin gray shirt
purple shorts   meant to make us the same

     but everyone could still tell who mattered

ABECEDARIAN FOR THE NUDE SCENE IN
LOVELY & AMAZING

Aspiring actress stands naked
before the man she bedded, asks him to
catalogue what's wrong. *You'd be*
doing me a favor. Six-minute scene,
Emily Mortimer's body scrutinized
from the front and the side.

                              I was that
girl, though I crossed my arms to
hide my breasts, sucked in, slouched.
I turned them down before they got the
joke out, though they usually weren't
kidding. I just thought they were.
Love me, I said with my eyes, sometimes
my mouth, but other times I said
nothing with nothing.

                                Your
opinion, Emily says, and he obliges. She
poses, six minutes. I pulled my
quilt to my chin, catalogued my own
reasons no one loved me. No need to
stand before a man and ask. I
touched my untouched stomach,
unspooled scarves from my sleeve, my
voice clearing the hurdle of my throat.
We all have our own reasons to cry,
X or
Y or
Z. This was mine. For now, at least.

ABECEDARIAN AT MY FATHER'S DEATHBED

At the movies the night he died. Make-
believe I wasn't. Put me in a
chair beside my mother, fitful
doze, magazine flip. My father's un-
even breathing, his
feeling something about to happen.
Go, he'd told me. The guilt. What if
he knew, sent me away? I can't
imagine the beeps, doctors
jostling my mother out the door. I
keep forgetting—my mother *and* me.
Liar. I can't make it real, can't put
myself in a room I left, can't make a
night be another night. I can
only watch not-myself, a character.
Picture *Grey's Anatomy*. Picture *ER*.
Quiet the soundtrack. My face un-
recognizable, prettier. Guest
star, one episode. That's all it
takes for a man to die.
Undo it. Not even his death, just the
vision of me in the theater,
wasting his last hour. Examine the
X-ray, find me where I wasn't—
yesterday, twenty-five years ago, a
zillion what-ifs, each of them torture.

THE PREACHER WITH MY FATHER'S NAME

When I used to look him up, he appeared: Jerry Fite, my father, died April 1998. It was like I conjured him. Like I called and he answered.

Once I found an October 1964 article in *The Lincoln Clarion* called "Peace Corpsman to Visit Lu; Taught . . ." and shared it with my mother and brother. The link is broken now; I don't know what the rest of the headline says. I know my father was in the Peace Corps for seven years—two in Tunisia, two as Sargent Shriver's executive secretary, three as the director of the Marianas District. But I won't find any photos of him I don't already have. I can't read his interviews. I liked to pretend I was the one asking him questions.

He wrote a progressive column that appeared in seven newspapers, from *The Meridian Star* in Mississippi to *The Springfield Daily News* in Massachusetts. Folded-up clippings tucked away in a fireproof box, only a fraction of what he wrote. When I try to find more, Google informs me there aren't many great matches for my search.

❋

When I look him up now, I find the preacher instead: Jerry Fite, no relation, still alive. My father's words gone. Replaced with a scroll of recorded sermons.

February 2023: "Biological male, gettin' naked in the women's locker room. Chaos!"

January 2023: "You can cancel the preacher, but you can't cancel the truth of God!"

December 2022: "She has a meek and quiet spirit. It's a tranquil spirit. Not that she doesn't talk—but she's not going to be wordy."

＊

When I was four, my father had a laryngectomy. I don't remember his voice. Only the whisper when he pressed a finger to the hole in his throat. When I was six, he had two major strokes. I remember his startled eyes as he tried to speak. He didn't go to church. Didn't want people looking at his cane.

He died when I was sixteen. No harps. No clouds. We buried his ashes. At his grave, the hole was small like he'd been a rabbit.

When I first discovered the preacher, my wild fear was my father had morphed into the living Jerry Fite. Was this deep voice anything like his? Is this what he would've looked like if he'd gotten old? Watching his sermons, I felt sick. Like I was sitting beside my father on our old orange couch, and when I kissed his cheek and pulled back, it was a stranger's face.

But those sermons aren't a portal to the afterlife. I don't believe in heaven. Or hell. I believe Whitman: *To die is different from what any one supposed, and luckier.* That man is not my father's reincarnated spirit. Not his contorted reflection. When I close the computer, easy as a coffin, he's nothing at all.

DECIPHERING GRIEF

His left palm blossomed all attention, stronger fist. The right's
messy handwriting. My father's fire gone from his whole right side.
When he died, my mother wore her grief like a nightgown
and rebounded with a monster. I unhooked myself from old definitions,
half-asleep like in the sitcom where someone snaps and says
Earth to Melissa. I stopped reading my horoscope; I didn't want to know.
I held a knife to my wrist but knew I was being dramatic,
trying to decipher like I was a character in English class.
My mother's face a full moon, white. How could I? Well,
how could she? I stayed in her house longer than I should have.
Better the devil you know. Better the shadows. Better the weeds.
We apologized twenty years later, balanced on either side
of our counselor whose job it was to see our story in the ashes of the blaze.

VIDEO STORE VILLANELLE

Everyone wandered the aisles of that video store,
before corporate shut it down, shut them all down,
shut down one more excuse to walk out our front doors.

Netflix existed, but trading one red envelope for
another couldn't compare to the little bell sound
of entering physical space. We wandered the store,

nodded at other wanderers. A metaphor
more than a place. A refuge in our small town,
the perfect excuse to walk out our front doors.

We stared at the backs of video cases, ignored
whatever realities we were trying to drown,
found better stories wandering the store,

Venice, the Alaskan wilderness, the North Shore,
not a hospital waiting room or our ex's Crown
Vic. We needed to walk through those doors

instead of visiting landmarks of every internal war.
Just to be somewhere, just to be gone, we came around,
wandered the aisles of the world's last video store.
Now we've run out of excuses to walk out our front doors.

COMMERCIAL TV

They all sold the girl I already was,
blonde and blue-eyed, destined
for big breasts, though who knew that
in the Baby Rollerblade days,
just a girl determined to jerk her way
across boardwalks and coffee tables,
everyone's mouth a perfect O
as she passed. Who is this girl, and why
doesn't she know to cross her arms
to hide her body? Barbie, my mom
didn't let me, I played with her
at my friend's house, dark-skinned
and beautiful, and when her mom
complimented my hair, called it golden,
my friend cried hers was like dirt.
In college, Britney sang Pepsi, close-up
her navel ring, close in on old men
in a home passing the oxygen, close on
Bob Dole telling his dog *Easy boy*.
She was 19, and she was for sale,
not the drink. I was 19, and I was
blonde and thin, breasts, men leering,
and still I wanted to be wanted more,
how to become the doll, plastic
stomach and smile that won't wipe away.

EASTER PANTOUM

My friends don't know their part in it. No alcohol, they assured,
so we went to the party, my alcoholic boyfriend and me.
Adult Easter egg hunt, slips of paper inside,
each with a drink order. Alcohol: the point of the party.

So my boyfriend and I went to the party.
That night, his hand over my mouth. That night,
after all those drink orders—the whole point—
he pinned me to his bedroom floor.

That night, his hand over my mouth. That night…
Each year, I decide to forget. Each year, I can't.
He pinned me to his bedroom floor.
Confession: I blame my friends as much as my rapist.

Each year, I decide to forget. Each year, I can't.
He felt remorse, he understood what he did—
unlike my friends, who blamed only him.
I last saw him at the public library five years ago.

When he saw me: remorse. He understood.
He lives in his car now, or at least he did
five years ago, last I saw him. He sat in a library chair
with no books, trying to stay warm. Winter.

Those friends and I live hours apart now.
I let them go in the unsatisfying way of hanging up a cell phone.
We still send holiday cards: warm winter wishes!
They don't know I let them go. We should catch up,

we say. We'll call. Unsatisfying, no closure.
Tonight: rainstorm. My husband and I
caught walking our dogs. The heavy clouds let it all go.
I wish I could. I wanted to forgive them by the end of this poem.

Tonight: my husband and I laughing in the rain.
Easter, again. More than twenty years later. Tonight: baptism.
I want to forgive them by the end of my life—
it's a beautiful life. My friends don't know their part in it.

PRETENTIOUS

My ex said, *So this is what the kids are listening to*,
Shakira at the height of her popularity.
My ex was twenty, so was I, certainly we were kids
in his car, listening to his music, bands no one knew,

by design. His design. I liked the radio,
summers at the pool, everyone singing in unison
with the speakers, sometimes someone aligned their dive
with the climax of the song. When in doubt,

who: if you're wrong, you're wrong; with *whom*,
you're wrong and pretentious. In my first book,
an incorrect word on purpose: *cul-de-sacs*, though I knew
proper *culs-de-sac*. I never want to seem superior,

put anyone in their place, their place is with me
in a movie theater, watching something everyone knows,
maybe *E. T.* Let's all adore tiny Drew Barrymore,
follow her career to *Scream*, we're all familiar

with that blonde bob. A student once called me
a know-it-all in his evaluation—my undoing.
Instead of wondering if he'd say that about a man,
I buried it inside my heart, made myself small as a stone.

MY PARANOIA CONSIDERS THE SONG I WROTE
AT AGE TEN

I took to my keyboard, wrote new lyrics for *Open Arms* by Journey,
though I didn't know it was *Open Arms* by Journey, I'd heard it
without realizing. Memory's so strange, I still mouth my words

instead of theirs: *Sometimes it feels like / I'm all alone. /
Nobody's there / when I come home.* Age ten, I wrote this,
living with two loving parents. I knew nothing of nobody there,

everybody there always, asking me to empty the dishwasher
or make my bed. What I longed for: solitude. I wrote the opposite.
I'm still writing the opposite, writing my father's death

into every poem, even this one, when my life now is so happy
I'm guilty about it. My loving husband. My three cute dogs
everyone we pass on walks agrees are cute. Shouldn't I stop

pretending just because poets are supposed to be sad?
*Sometimes it feels like / I won't die alone. / My husband's there /
when I come home.* Even at ten I knew—no one wants to hear that shit.

SEPTEMBER 11, 2001

I woke with my boyfriend beside me in my mother's house,
after a night of sex, though I don't remember the sex,
we just never went a night without it, once for my birthday
I asked for an innocence day, holding hands and kissing
without tongue so I could feel cherished as a person
instead of desired as a body I didn't even feel comfortable in
and he could not give me that gift. I dressed in clean clothes
and he put on whatever he'd come over in and I drove him
to work, I drove him everywhere, his license revoked,
DUI going out for pizza in the middle of the night when
I'd begged him to get delivery. We did not turn on the TV
as we dressed. We listened to a CD in the car. After I dropped him
in the Applebee's parking lot, I drove to my 9:30 class and
our professor had borrowed one of those rolling TVs and it was on.

I GO BACK TO APRIL 2004
after Sharon Olds

I see us sitting in a church pew, I see the knot
of your tie, tip of your boutonniere,
your dark eyes all pupil,
your face unwhiskered, chin scar
exposed, car accident, I see my throat slashed
by the bottom edge of the photo, a before-selfie
selfie on a disposable camera, my eyes
thick black smears, my chin raised,
we look down, we unsmile,
this photograph a reckoning. We are
at a wedding, my mother and her abusive partner's,
I refused to go and you said I'd regret it
but you'll be there, and this gesture
solidifies our eight-month relationship.
During the ceremony, my mother
scans the room to find me
among only five guests, everyone disapproves,
I've never cried so hard but you hold my hand,
and in the car later we make our own promises,
one promise not to have a child,
who might have been conceived tonight,
not to pass down old hurts,
to let our love be enough.
Unlike the couple marrying tonight,
their divorce three years later,
we will be together until death.
I sit in the pew, watch my mother kiss the man
who cheated and left, cheated and left,
the man she always welcomed back, and I think,
Do what you are going to do, and I will tell about it.

WALT WHITMAN CALLED 37 A BEGINNING

"I, now thirty-seven years old in perfect health begin,
Hoping to cease not till death."

37, Mr. Ortolani taught English the year my father died.
Leaves of Grass instead of going to his grave.

37, Sharon Olds published her first book. *Satan Says*
at the coffee shop where I wrote my first terrible poems.

37, my brother collapsed in the hallway—*Too late*,
for a job he loved, a woman. He had to travel to the past.

37, I finally left my hometown.
37, Sylvia Plath dead seven years.

37, my mother pregnant in a sundress.
37, my father didn't have a daughter, or a dream of a daughter.

PART TWO

MY STUDENTS READ MY CHART TO ME

They tell me my moon is so Sagittarius, they can just tell

        I don't know what that means, I say

  They sigh

How can I know so much about Elizabeth Bennet
    without considering her chart

        Do we know when Elizabeth Bennet was born?

No but obviously she's such a Taurus
With a Libra moon
Aries rising
Yeah exactly

    Last 15 min of class   Fourth quarter   Seniors

        OK   how can you tell about my moon

They say I have warm energy
I draw people in

    One student looks into her computer like it's a crystal ball

She has my whole chart here

    Totally unselfconscious
    Totally upright in her chair
    Totally unlike me at her age

She reads me only good things   only what she says applies

inspirational   storyteller   humble

I thought Leos were supposed to be brash

Surprisingly humble, she amends

Obviously I don't know their signs   only that I love them
            and they're leaving   spinning out of my orbit

It's like this every year

A STUDENT STOPS BY MY CLASSROOM

to say goodbye. Winter break. An hour later, we're still talking.
She reminds me of me. She sees it, too. Sometimes
she's the only one laughing when I hoped the whole class would.
I don't have a daughter. Don't know what it's like to have a daughter.

She asks where she should go to college.
The whole time she's talking she's fiddling with her bag.
It won't zip. I tell her I can't tell her, but I know
there's no one right choice. Many paths to happiness. She says

she'd go local but it won't impress anyone. She knows
that sounds awful but if she's being honest. I tell her I'm not sure
I wanted to be Kansas Poet Laureate. I wanted to be important.
No one's impressed by high school teacher. They say *Wow, so noble*,

but . . . She nods. She gets it. She's thinking of becoming a lawyer
so maybe she'll be her parents' favorite. She laughs like it's a joke.
Finally the bag zips. I tell her please keep me posted,
I'm invested. She says she will. I don't have a daughter. This is not that.

THE GAP

I wear my new boots with dresses to school
like Claire Danes in *My So-Called Life*

which I rewatched recently   which totally holds up

     though what did I ever see in Jordan? Obviously
     Rickie Vasquez the real treasure here

I mentioned this show to my students
who never know what I'm talking about

             Yesterday I said Hi Sam
             to my student Sam
             and then made the guitar sound
             that accompanies Sam's ladder
             on *Clarissa Explains It All*

It stars Melissa Joan Hart   I explained
She's *Sabrina the Teenage Witch*

      which also meant nothing

My students wear Doc Martens
but have never seen *90210*

          They do not understand

Donna's father was literally Doc Martin   They did not cry

     when Luke Perry died   though they know him
       from *Riverdale*

He's just the dad
He's not the most beautiful boy in the world

And I said Excuse me
Google Imaged that white T-shirt
those sideburns
that slow smile

My job is to teach them

MANDY MOORE CANCELS THE REST OF HER SUMMER TOUR SO WE HAVE A MANDY MOORE MARATHON INSTEAD

for M.K.

If we weren't going to sing *I Wanna Be with You*
with Mandy Moore in an intimate venue, we needed
to rewatch *Chasing Liberty*, the superior President's daughter
dating a Secret Service man movie, of which there are three.

We needed the movies no one would call her movies—
Princess Diaries was Anne Hathaway's, *Saved* Jena Malone's.
But they were her movies, at least to us. Mandy Moore
changed our lives. My therapist said to make two lists:

why he isn't good enough, why a fictional character is.
Shane West in *A Walk to Remember*. My boyfriend
would never have driven me to the state line
so I could be in two places at once, let alone married me

in the church my parents were married in before I died
of leukemia, though he did take me to get a tattoo,
a real one, not a press-on he blew on all sexily in the car.
Would I have left if I hadn't sat alone in that theater, sobbing?

And you—Fan club, unfolded poster. You memorized
each of her looks in the *Candy* video: Pink T-shirt and braids.
Red tank, hair down. Yellow spaghetti straps, headphones.
Who said you had to love Shane West? Couldn't you love her?

IN OUR SMALL HOUSE ONLY A WALL SEPARATES US

In the kitchen my husband replaces the faucet,
sprayer coiled like a can of snakes. I strain to hear
his movements. He's working quietly because
I'm building something, too, this line

and this one, the space between. Sometimes
I diminish my work. Not practical at all,
looking out the window and trying to guess
what our neighbor will pull from his trunk

(a box of Corona!); imagining a split screen
of my husband, now spackling a small hole
in the wall, and our neighbor, lining bottles
in his fridge. My husband doesn't drink

as he used to, nineteen years ago when we met.
Back then he punctuated every sentence
with a cigarette. People assume our reason
for being childless: living like we're twenty

forever. But oatmeal for breakfast, stretches
before bed, subtitled TV. We have settled
comfortably into forty. Our neighbor's our age.
Sometimes he drinks while his children

spring from their trampoline into the sky.
We wave as we all sit to dinner in our backyards.
My husband cooks every night, a poem
we can eat. After, I wash dishes in our new sink.

MORNING ABECEDARIAN WITH DOGS

All three dogs
burrowed under our
chins. All three
dogs growl at the alarm.
Eventually, coffee and
fruit. We delay
going out, but look
how happy
it makes them,
jockeying for first out the
kitchen door, running
laps in the cold.
Muddy paws, but I
never mind wiping them—
oh, they stand so
patiently, barely
quivering as they
raise one leg, then another.
Shower. Dress in
the dark. Rush rush
until you walk into my
view, kiss me goodbye.
We can forget,
X-ing off to-do lists,
yawning, but this is the
zenith of our lives. Yes, this.

SLOWDOWN VILLANELLE

I don't want a dishwasher. He doesn't want a riding mower.
The lavender dish soap, the grooves in the grass: meditation.
For a while, no talk or thought. Summer's slower

pace. I worry the wand into each glass. I lower
each bowl into its baptism. Our dishes a congregation
drying on the rack. No dishwasher. No riding mower.

Sunday dusk, the yard his chapel. He waves at churchgoers
driving by. The mower his pulpit, his standing ovation.
For a while, no talk or thought. Summer's slower

schedule. No more wrenching another task inside an hour.
Let this one linger. Let the darkening sky invite revelation.
Why would anyone want a dishwasher or riding mower?

I watch him in the window, then myself when it turns mirror.
He comes inside, presses against me in the kitchen.
For a while, no talk or thought. Summer's slower

evenings. No rush to brush our teeth or shower.
I pour each of us a glass of wine. A little communion.
Our work done, hand-washing dishes, pushing the mower,
we talk for hours. Our life as full as anyone's, just slower.

OUTDOOR CONCERT POEM

for A.C. & O.E.

Hoodie weather poem. Mouthing the wrong words poem. Cheap beer poem, no wine at this venue poem. Drunk guy going gospel poem, hands in the air poem. Our best friend laughing poem. Us laughing poem. Our teenage godson refusing to laugh poem. Sunset poem. Relief clouds after a rainstorm poem. No longer necessary sunglasses poem, people wearing them just to be cool poem. Someone finally complimenting our Stone Cold Steve Austin blanket poem. Merch line poem. Bathroom line poem. Canned music between bands poem. Our godson knows all these 90s songs poem, his mom raising him right poem. Totally dark now poem. All sunglasses off poem, no one can see how cool we are or aren't now poem. The band we came to see poem. Mouthing the right words poem. Shouting the right words at our cringing godson poem. Close our eyes for this one poem. Contact high poem. Drum solo poem. Lead singer shouting out the wrong city poem. Dancing on the lawn poem. Encore poem.

HOW DARE ANYONE SAY I DON'T KNOW LOVE

because I never prayed to the ceiling and pushed
    because I never held a hybrid you-me

and named it

    (Unconceived ghost   I can almost see dancing
        barefoot in sprinkler mist

        beautiful dream I've never wanted)

    People explain   my sad life to me
    People explain   dogs are not children

How dare anyone say I don't know what I'm missing

    They don't know what they're missing

our bed not quite an island
            our bed a peninsula

       We slip into sleep   instead of making dinner
       (We order in   We linger)

I don't post this love   because not everyone has it
I don't poem this love   private drawer

                quiet corner

    They don't know what they're missing

           our matador hearts
        our greenhouse love

NOT-MOTHER GHAZAL

Small toys from your mother's pale egg-
shell purse: pink-eared bunny, silly putty egg.

Remember the chickens at the old house, broody
and trying to will life into unfertilized eggs.

Say you're a robin. Say you're a mother-
to-be, sturdy nest and five shining eggs.

You can't stop the brown-headed cowbird from
swapping a perfect blue oval for an egg.

Kitchen tinged with batter and grease. A lid
uncovered and recovered, the cracking of an egg.

Colonizing pans, spreading like fear, waiting
in a petri dish, hopeful sibling eggs.

For your cousin, syringes and shots. For her,
surgery. A list of names and all your eggs.

Melissa, you are not your elegant mother.
You are not a mother at all. A year of wasted eggs.

FAMILY OF ORIGIN

There's a picture of all four of us, photographer unknown. I'd clearly woken everyone up and my mother looks so happy, truly, no sarcasm, to be midnight awake. Her hand prompts my brother's arm; can't he be happy too? His face, age eleven, the face of my students now. My blanket white, my onesie white, I am the sun he blinks from.

❀

My house with my husband is quiet. Right now the only sound is the eye click, the tail flick, of Felix the clock. It turns out quiet is what I've spent my whole life searching for. The air conditioner wakes up and I let out a breath I hadn't known I was holding.

❀

My birth yanked my brother from one tumultuous childhood to another. After me, our father's cancer, his strokes. Before me, our father's drinking. He took my brother on ride-alongs to the dump to haul off liquor bottles so Dad's parents wouldn't see, so they'd keep on thinking he was perfect like I would, keep on blaming Mom like I would.

❀

Today my brother posted "Happy heavenly birthday, Dad" and I posted nothing.

My mom's comment on my brother's post: "Oh how precious! That made me cry."

My mom's comment to me: _____, in response to
_____.

Which was the point. Anything I post gets an outpour, and he's been gone
25 years. I want to spend his birthday in the quiet. I want to poem not post.

❉

My brother got the divorce, which lasted only a year. Mom's ultimatum:
booze or her, and Dad chose booze. Then her, when he got sober. Before
their divorce, Dad kept Mom up raving about politics. She couldn't nod hard
enough to stop him. Yes yes, she was outraged too, but they had to teach in
three hours. He wouldn't let her sleep.

❉

Death and guilt have made my father perfect in my memories and poems.
I know he wasn't, but in my lifetime all he did was type what I narrated
to him before his strokes; try to narrate to me after. In my lifetime he was
pretty close.

Finally I believe my memories are mine to write, but can I write my
mother's, my brother's? They were a family of three for eleven years before
me. Secondhand stories I strain to remember like last night's dream.

BUS RIDE

A break from the heat, though the AC relief
lasts only a few minutes before

I take it for granted. Feels like nothing now.
We pass a school I didn't attend, a life

I didn't live. We pass my friend's college dorm,
where I stayed sometimes, a guest or a ghost.

Even when I close my eyes, sunlight persists.
A guy boards, soaked in cologne

that doesn't remind me of anyone. We pass
the speed limit sign, 40, like all signs this year.

POEM WITH THREE ENDINGS

My student asks *What does this have to do with anything?*
as I tell the story of my father dying. I stammer.

We must be vulnerable but we must be ready. Earn it.
Next semester I'll be someone else, cool and tall,

not hunched like my mother who finally succeeded
in folding in on herself, making herself small.

What does this have to do with anything? This is why
we're here—to live and to die, for someone to care.

What does this have to do with anything? Get out.
Have the counselor put you in Comparative Myth.

What does this have to do with anything? In this poem,
record him. Let him read it and feel something like shame.

FORTY

Ordering tea from a former student, we discuss
a concert she drove to Chicago to see, a band

she thought I wouldn't know, a band I love.
When I sit with my drink, she plays their CD

and we smile from across the room, from across
the years. I came to this same coffee shop at her age,

wrote behind the window, wondered if I'd marry,
become a teacher, where I'd live. Strange to know

those answers. Like I know the answer to every
question about my life. Like I time traveled to find out.

ODE TO ARRIVING AT THE PLACE JUST BEFORE IT OPENS

It invites awkwardness, standing in a clump with others
wondering if maybe we should be in a line instead, after all

so-and-so was here first and what if
the mechanic/cashier/pizza place proprietor can't tell?

Then more awkwardness, throat clearing and hitchhiker's thumb,
though honestly why do we fear awkwardness? Why be wary

of the old man leaning on his truck commenting on
the early bird's worm? Well I know why, and so does my husband,

whose truck sparked my car to life before dropping me off,
he calls to make sure the man is not dangerous

or condescending, and though the man writes the name and address
of another car shop in case this one can't help me, I consider

this kindness, his asking where I'm from, his telling where he's from
and his decades-long history with this shop, he could be

every mechanic's father or grandfather. He does not
pull out his phone, so neither do I, neither do those who join us.

We end up talking about our dogs, and whose day isn't better
upon learning one woman's dog weighs only three pounds?

Though I must admit I also enjoy when a waiting group
does pull out phones, the scooching silently to make room,

the not wanting to make a big deal of it, the wordless thank you,
usually a nod. Nice just to notice someone's shoes or glasses,

especially if you need new shoes or glasses. Nice just to feel
everyone's getting ready energy, the small subtle changes in the air,

adjusting a purse strap, shifting weight, when we hear
that small click of a door unlocking and we know we are welcome inside.

WHAT THIS MORNING NEEDS

Even on Saturdays, the list stirs me,
not actually the list but the guilt,
planning, grading, making someone wait
an extra day, a week, my old principal said

imagine these students closing Taco Bell,
babysitting siblings, 2 a.m. Red Bull
sponsoring this essay, and you make them wait?
No alarm but the one in my bloodstream.

My husband's hand on my arm.
He says, *What this morning needs is Tom Waits.*
Then *Downtown Train*, growl and urge
from his phone. I stay, try to stay,

in the moment, close my eyes,
travel with him to our first date, a song
like this one, maybe this exact song,
on his truck radio. My husband nudges

a dog into my arms so I can't email a parent.
He says, *You are determined to ruin this morning.*
Then *Hold On*, plaintive and low.
Finally, I give my phone to the nightstand,

the dogs between us, their little sighs
so quiet you miss them if you're not quiet, too.
We hold the dogs, mouth the words
when we know them, linger in the sun-sheets.

WALT WHITMAN PROMISES ME THE ORIGIN OF ALL POEMS

"Stop this day and night with me and you shall possess the origin of all poems."

My husband has cleaned the aquarium and now
new water drips the tank. The fish

accept this baptism. I am trying to write
the present. Now my husband makes dinner.

I keep following him into rooms
just as he leaves them. This is not tragedy.

Comedy, the comings and goings,
misunderstandings. The dog left my side,

and in those five words, he returned. The present
is impossible, the basketball on TV hovering

between sets of begging hands. The oven
feeling of use after sitting empty all day.

My book lost until my husband found it
on the shelf right where it should be, now open

to page 26. I am trying to write the present.
A quiet night, a photo of a moment

I wouldn't think to photograph. Isn't this
the origin of all poems? The blink, the breath.

Jump shot, open page. Kitchen table,
placemats and napkins. The before bedtime—

dishwater and wine. Letting the dogs out
once more. The fish now settled in the quiet dark.

PART THREE

I GOT OFF THE PLANE AND EVERYONE WAS DEAD

Betty White, whose secrets to a long life
I read to my husband in the airport hours earlier:
a cocktail before dinner, cockeyed optimism.

And a guy from high school, who once raped
my husband's friend. People are posting the usual
glows, as if he were as beloved as Betty White,

and to some he was. We're all something else
to someone else. Maybe he became better, a person
who hated sharing a body with the person he used to be.

I don't know how he died, only that he was
my age, not weeks from 100 like Betty White,
who reminds me I might not be halfway through,

who reminds me how much my classmate lost.
How much my husband's friend lost, who died
this year, too. I'm used to grandparents dying,

my father, aunts and uncles, and now I guess it's us,
rare and tragic but not like when my students die,
a dozen in sixteen years, a small percentage,

but tell that to their parents. Tell it to my classmate's
father, my English professor who taught a class
on Whitman and cried each time he read aloud.

MIDLIFE ABECEDARIAN

At the antique mall with a friend,
buried in a bin: a Florence Griffith Joyner doll,
comes with a full set of nail stickers. I read once that
during a race her nail flew off; after it
ended she walked the track to
find it. Her miniature wears a one-legged bodysuit, neon
green and pink, the detail I most associate with
her. My friend asks if she's still alive. I look
it up—no, 1998, seizure in her sleep,
just before her 39th birthday. I only now, in midlife,
know how young that is to die. When I was
little, forty was my father's scratchy cheek,
my mother's face cream. Forty was inevitable. Death had
not yet entered my mind, though soon I'd learn. My
old babysitter, my classmate whose father skidded
past the stop sign one winter, Anne Frank, Titanic, I couldn't
quit learning death. I'm still learning it,
researching even the slightest
symptoms, wondering each birthday how much more
time. I set down Flo-Jo's cardboard home. My friend holds
up another doll. I look this one up too, déjà
vu, only she's alive, Billie Jean King,
white tennis dress with blue Peter Pan collar,
x number of years left. Next month, I'll turn forty. Well—
you never really know. I *should*. 4-0. In tennis, the
zero is love. 40-love. I would love to turn forty.

ORDINARY MAGIC

The December our dog died, my husband and I gave up
decorating. Seven years ago. No kids, no pressure
for our home to be magical. Just ordinary magic now—

a robin's nest beside our breakfast, mother's dive missions
beneath pinecones and leaves, every backyard secret,
unearthing worms for her fugitive babies.

Sometimes, reading my old poems,
I want to give up. How embarrassing, trying so hard
to arrange the world into words. Next door,

a couple younger than we are call for their kids.
They emerge, every backyard secret. One leaps
from the swing set. I wish someone would snap a photo midair.

ODE TO THE TV REWATCH PODCAST MY FRIEND
AND I STARTED OVER THE PANDEMIC
for C.H.

He and I watched TV together, in separate
time zones. Kansas, New York. My husband heard us

dissecting and suggested it. We talked for hours
before we even recorded. Fear:

Mine—online school forever.
His—Broadway shut down forever.

After we anxiety spiraled the future, we lost ourselves
in someone else's story. We picked

comfort TV (*Parenthood*) and alliteration (*Parenthood Pals*).
Nearly three years later we are struggling to find time.

Back then we were drowning in time, staring down the barrel
of time. Only six more episodes. We are seeing it through.

Listeners in Germany and Holland. One listener sent us
a video of herself playing Christmas songs on her accordion.

I cried thinking of vulnerability, hers and mine,
how pandemic loneliness brought us

into each other's living rooms. I'm a poet. I forget
process over product. I wonder

who will publish the poem while I'm writing it
and then the poem's no good. We sign off:

May God bless and keep you always.
May your wishes all come true.

Because it's the *Parenthood* theme song. Not because
we believe. We don't know. Bob Dylan only pretended to know.

I WAS NOT PREPARED FOR THIS VAL KILMER
DOCUMENTARY

I'm remembering more than watching
a man, golden in videos and photographs.
It can seem he only ever existed that way.

Time blinks and now he speaks
pressing a finger to a hole in his throat.
I'd never noticed the resemblance,

my dad's breath, Val's breath, so heavy
rattling from that hole, which
my dad covered with a gauze flap, which

Val covers with scarves. Each time Val goofs
for the camera, a gesture or wink, it jolts—
did I forget my father's humor? Hilarious,

even after the laryngectomy, the strokes.
I think of pain when I think of him,
his and mine. Never a real conversation.

Would he walk me down the aisle?
He died before we'd find out.
When Val smiles to himself before

seeing his adult daughter, also his neighbor—
they sort of bow on their respective stoops—
it's so cute I could cry, and then I do, I really do.

SELF-PORTRAIT WITH SCAR

It's true that I'm young, and it's true that I'm old.
Ask my mother; ask my students. My mother's
headache: giant cell arteritis. My student's dizzy spell:

tumor. Since I can't get a whole body scan
every year—WebMD. This morning, dry patch
or skin cancer. Last week, healthy tongue images.

Last month, enamel erosion. One summer,
I drove a relative to get dentures. The next summer,
I drove another. Each in my passenger seat,

gauze and blood, heads tipped back
like they were gargling saltwater or talking to God.
I thought the spot on my front tooth meant I was

losing my front tooth, but the dentist polished it away
in thirty seconds. Two hours ago I downloaded
a flashlight so I could shine my throat for strep.

Once a cold lingered so I thought maybe COVID.
Once a cold lingered so I thought maybe HIV.
Something is coming—death, eventually

or soon, not recognizing myself in the mirror. Once
I carved a whitehead from my forehead with nail scissors.
Now I look up whether scars ever go away on their own.

NEW YEAR'S EVE

No more resolutions. Too much
pressure. I quit. Time is sand
slipping through
the plastic hourglasses
in Boggle and Taboo,
names that seem ominous now.
I used to live for others.
I bought into a curated timeline.
Time is sand slipping through
my bare legs—box,
not beach. Backyard view,
not ocean or mountain. Cable-knit,
not cashmere. I no longer want
fantasy. I want real. I want true.
Finally, I love my life
as it is. But time is sand
slipping through my fingers.
I can't stop it. Oh, how I want to.

MY BROTHER POSTS A PHOTO

Five men at the VFW, arms around each other.
Two men hold beers, my brother

and his friend who died, this photo a tribute,
a detail my mom missed when she hit the heart.

My immunocompromised mother
and unvaccinated brother haven't seen each other

in years. The three of us will never again
visit my father's grave together

in Dadeville, MO, pop. 220,
where drivers waved when we passed.

Under the photo, someone asks
what happened. Someone asks COVID.

My brother writes *Not sure,* which I'm sure
means yes. All five men look right into the camera.

HEREDITARY

At a funeral, an old woman asks what's wrong.
I'm furious. My brother just says what's wrong,

cerebral palsy. He balances as best he can.
He trails behind. I link my arm through his,

carry his plate to the table, but
don't make a big deal. I'd do it for anyone.

His biological mother died giving birth.
He didn't get enough oxygen.

The stress he must've felt just becoming.
What we pass on, even without shared blood.

Our father trailed behind after his strokes.
I linked my arm through his. I carried his plate.

MOTHER SESTINA

Your hands, invisible
under your hair,
shells over your ears.
I can't hear you.
Even now you are six
around your mother.

Your mother
is becoming invisible.
She's 76—
morning pills, thinning hair.
She walks right past you,
whispers nothing in your ear.

She never wore ear-
rings, lipstick. This mother
stunned you
subtly—invisible
makeup, undone hair.
More beautiful at 56

than some women at 36.
Your hands cover your ears—
those pills mean nothing. Her hair
isn't thinning. Your mother
isn't inching toward an invisible
circle on the calendar. You

forget death, drinking your
coffee, reading the news, six

a.m. It's there, an invisible
deadline in your ear—
your mother
won't be in your hair

forever. Thinning hair.
Morning pills. You
will lose your mother,
as you lost your father at six-
teen. Put your ear
to the phone. She isn't invisible.

Your mother used to comb your hair,
invisible snags that made you
cry. You were six. She soothed into your ear.

REWATCHING *REBEL WITHOUT A CAUSE*

The opening at juvenile hall. The red jacket.
The bonkers scene with the glass bottle of milk:
he swigs, he cradles, he presses the glass
against his forehead, cold compress.
The absolute absence of memory of such a scene.
You'd seen this movie, you know you had,
but it wasn't your nostalgia, it was your mother's.
The way she talked of James Dean's death,
Natalie Wood's death, like they were her friends.
The car. The boat. The decades between,
the decades since. The way she clutched her jacket
closed last time you saw her, in May, only a little chilly.

MARATHON
for J.J.

Her kids ask how long we'll be
watching *Clueless*

                                         Brittany Murphy dead
                                         Paul Rudd untouched by time

She says   Do you know what a marathon is
It's one movie after another   all night long

                          Even after we're in bed   they ask

Yes   she says   even then

      She sets them up in the kitchen with screens

10 Things I Hate About You next   Heath Ledger dead
                                         Julia Stiles elusive

      After bedtime   extra stories and songs

She's All That

                                         Paul Walker dead
                                         Rachael Leigh Cook
                                         in the Netflix remake

Single dad in each movie

                             mother dead
                  freak accident during a routine liposuction
                  or leukemia
                            or gone
                  leaving two daughters
                  one set of pearls

but their mom is just with me   in the basement
staring at the darkened ceiling   sky without stars
                                       like we used to when we mapped our lives

WHEN MACAULAY CULKIN WAS THE WORLD'S BIGGEST STAR

I was rinsing my filmy watercolor cup,
having carried that morning's sunrise with me
into 4th grade art. We all got two plastic columns

of Easter egg colors, and a brush that scratched
against the paint. No one was counting on me
for box office gold, just not to spill

onto my neighbor's paper. I feel like
I know Macaulay Culkin, as if being children
at the same time means we grew up together.

In this way I also know the Columbine shooters,
all of us seniors. When they were killing,
when their lives were ending, I was in AP Spanish,

on a day when half the class was absent
so we played Trivial Pursuit (in English).
Eric Harris is still 18, Dylan Klebold 17.

And Macaulay Culkin is alive, but he's ten
forever, red sweater and toy rifle strap. I am 41.
No one tells me they can't believe I'm 41. They can.

DOUBLING

I am not yet born. The nest pulses with weight and demand. I can't sunflower my head to the light with no proof. Upturn my eyes. Everyone on the right path is moving through a garden to a front door.

❀

I am five and in my childhood living room. Hush the lights. What do I do in that room? I turn into myself. Only let the chandelier tips burn. Wind it like the music box, slowly, imagine it unspooling from the ceiling, crashing down. Let the room become carousel. Shadows puppet the walls and I wonder if they are themselves, and if not, what it would take for them to get back home.

❀

I am ten and dripping glitter onto construction Valentines. *Godverdomme*, Oma yells, my only Dutch word. Her faucet beeps when her glass fills. Her blind eyes see everything. I, too, will go old, use my hands as eyes.

❀

I am twenty and single and want to cover up. I am sheeny and dripping in the corner farthest from the toilet. I love boys more than myself. I hand them my journals and say knock yourselves out. I watch them walk. Their coats over my shoulders, I can never shrug away. A house flickers past, window eyes, door mouth, but not the right house; a stick figure man, tall and faceless, holds my hand. I dream of love, and after I find love, I thank God, though I don't believe in God.

❀

I am forty and married to someone who will someday become a tree in our backyard. My ribs want the white picket fence, but they poke wrought iron. I can't squeeze my fingers tight enough. I am afraid of losing all I have. Even now. Or—not losing it, but not deserving it. I write poems in the living room but he waltzes through with the Swiffer, pours water into pots. I can't be counted on even to wash the morning's fruit. He is useful and I am not. In the garden of the body there are weeds, and all I can do is pull. He plants. He creates life and I create words.

✳

I'll be eighty soon and widowed. Or dead—maybe I'll be the tree. My hands are outlines, invisible leaves veining. When the chimney spools gray, I dream blue ocean and sky. Remember Oma in her bathing cap, surfing Ormond Beach? God is a mouth gone, a sheet propped up by air, a branch with no bird perched. God is a glass drying on the counter. Shadows puppet themselves against curtains. I become shadow, mount the wall and join them, seize the flame shape as I would horse's hair.

THIS IS THE POEM IN WHICH I RETIRE FROM POETRY

Chekhov's gun, heavy and metallic: no metaphor.
Decoration, wall hanging, never meant to burst the room

with sound. I won't be appreciated in my time.
I won't be appreciated in another time. Play the set,

no encore. Only right answers, please. More
grammar lessons for my students. Bun my hair, pencil

my skirts. Poetry's a phase and everyone who gave it up
in college was right. Move to the horizon

with the ship, everyone on the dock witnessing
my transformation from poet to dot. Change my name

to Jennifer, also a popular name the year I was born.
Dye my hair brown. Wave a black cloak and duck, poof.

LET'S SAY THE AFTERLIFE IS REAL

It helps. My mother and I visit my father's grave,
her name next to his. Is it a comfort
that my father is waiting, here if nowhere else?
Half of him anyway, the other half
buried somewhere else. My mother wants
to be halved, too, split between her loves,
first and last. Ashes, I should mention,
not sawed in half like the girl on stage waving
from her coffin. I am trying to mourn now,
as if I could ease the load for my future self.
My mother becomes an expression,
walking over her own grave, her future,
her lack of a future. Every blade of grass bristles.

WALT WHITMAN WRITES MY EPITAPH

"And to die is different from what any one supposed, and luckier."

My husband laughed at the idea.
Don't you think it's beautiful? I asked.

Oh yes, he said. But it's an epitaph
for a person at peace with dying, not you.

When Uncle Jerry jolted awake and found
his family in his room, expecting him to die

the day before he died, that look—
I'll never forget. Panic. A genie

who wanted birthed back into the bottle.
Choose the devil we know, this horrible world,

over the possible paradise we don't.
I don't want heaven. I want my dogs to live

a hundred years, my husband
puppeting their arms (yes, arms) in bed

to make me laugh on weekend mornings.
I love my life every single day,

a not-very-poetic thing to admit, I admit,
and to die is exactly what everyone supposes.

NOTES

"Generation Catalano" is a term coined by *Teen Vogue* editor Danielle Nussbaum to capture those born between 1977 and 1981. For more on this, read Doree Shafrir's 2011 *Slate* article "Generation Catalano: The Generation Stuck between Gen X and the Millennials."

"I Go Back to April 2004" is after Sharon Olds' "I Go Back to May 1937," and its italicized final line is also the final line in Olds' poem.

The epigraphs from the three Walt Whitman poems are all from "Song of Myself."

The band in "Outdoor Concert Poem" is Weezer. The band in "Forty" is Pinegrove.

The italicized line in "Marathon" is a quote from *Clueless*.

The coffee shop mentioned in several poems is La Prima Tazza in Lawrence, KS.

ACKNOWLEDGMENTS

Many thanks to the editors of the journals in which these poems first appeared, sometimes in earlier versions or with different titles:

3 Elements Review: "Ordinary Magic"

DIAGRAM: "Abecedarian for the Nude Scene in *Lovely & Amazing*"

Drunk Monkeys: "Mother Sestina" and "When Macaulay Culkin Was the World's Biggest Star"

Elysium Review: "How Dare Anyone Say I Don't Know Love"

HAD: "I Was Not Prepared for This Val Kilmer Documentary," "My Students Read My Chart to Me," and "New Year's Eve"

Harbor Review: "Not-Mother Ghazal"

Ilanot Review: "Let's Say the Afterlife Is Real" (Orison Books' *Best Spiritual Literature Anthology* nominee) and "My Paranoia Considers the Song I Wrote at Age Ten"

KANSAS! Magazine: "Morning Abecedarian with Dogs"

Kansas City Voices: "Walt Whitman Called 37 a Beginning," "Walt Whitman Promises Me the Origin of All Poems," and "Walt Whitman Writes My Epitaph"

Lines + Stars: "Self-Portrait with Scar"

Pleiades: "Deciphering Grief" and "A Student Stops by My Classroom"

Ploughshares: "A Man I Didn't Sleep with Asked What Word Defined Me" and "Speechless"

Porcupine Literary: "The Gap" and "Poem with Three Endings"

Rejection Letters: "This Is the Poem in Which I Retire from Poetry"

Rise Up Review: "The Preacher with My Father's Name"

Rogue Agent: "Easter Pantoum"

Shō Poetry Journal: "I Got off the Plane and Everyone Was Dead"

SWWIM: "Midlife Abecedarian" (Pushcart Prize nominee)

Ways: "*Before Sunrise* on the VCR"

West Trade Review: "Abecedarian at My Father's Deathbed"

Sections of "Walking Sonnet" were published separately in different forms in the journals *Flint Hills Review, Major 7th Magazine*, and *Whale Road Review*.

"Hereditary" first appeared in the anthology *Braving the Body*, edited by Nicole Callihan, Pichchenda Bao, and Jennifer Franklin, and published by Harbor Editions.

"Bus Ride," selected for the 2024 Lawrence Transit Poet Laureate program, was featured on an electric city bus in Lawrence, KS.

THANKS

One of my favorite poems is Linda Pastan's "25th High School Reunion," the last lines of which serve as an epigraph for this book. *Midlife Abecedarian* is coming out 25 years after my own high school graduation, and I'm realizing that—as a poet, at least—I really have turned into myself. I used to think the point of all this was to try to impress people so I'd feel validated and like I was enough. Now I understand that the point of all this is love—working with people I love, writing what I love, supporting poets I love. Nothing else matters.

Thank you, first of all, to Courtney LeBlanc. I'm so glad we took a chance on each other back in 2020, when *Green* became the first book Riot in Your Throat ever published. This time around, we know exactly what we have in each other. You are my publisher turned dear friend, which isn't a relationship I knew existed or would've thought possible. I adore our origin story.

Thank you to my best friend, Jai Johnson, for designing not only this cover, but all my books' covers, including the handcrafted self-published book we made together more than twenty years ago, before I knew that anyone else would ever publish me. Thank you to Meryl Carver-Allmond for taking not only this author photo, but all my author photos, as well as my previous books' cover photos. If video stores still existed, I would've gone to you for this cover too. Thank you to Shanna Compton for the impeccable interior book design, for both *Green* and *Midlife Abecedarian.* Thank you to Lynn Melnick for shaping this book into what it was meant to be.

Thank you to the poetry communities that have given me a place to belong. Thank you to the Pittsburg poets—these are the first poems you didn't directly workshop, but your influence is forever. Thank you to the December poets—you are the reason there are only three years between the last book and this one. Thank you to the brunch poets—you've taught me that there's no need to feel intimidated by poets I admire, that I should just love you and let you love me. And thank you to Ruth Williams—the two of us became a community of our own over the pandemic, and it's one of the richest relationships of my life.

In this book, I write about things I never let myself before, like being a high school teacher. My bio used to state that I lived and taught in Kansas; I wanted people to assume I taught at a university, that I was an academic, and I didn't mind hiding who I was to make that happen. For a long time, I thought my profession meant I wasn't a real poet. Thank you to the community of teacher poets I respect so much—especially Joan Kwon Glass, Laura Passin, and Leah Umansky—for helping me reframe how I see myself and my life's work. For helping me realize that I love being a high school teacher, and what a lucky thing that is. I'm so glad finally to be writing poems for and about my students.

Thank you to my friends, especially those of you I've dedicated poems to in this book, for the support and conversations and movie marathons. Thank you to my family for understanding that writing our stories in the most honest way I know how is meant to honor you. I love you completely, the hard parts too, and it's how I want to be loved in return.

Most of all, thank you to Marc Johnson. Because of you, I know what it means to be acknowledged. To be championed. To feel like the best in the world. These are, of course, wrestling references. You've brought me into your weird world, and I've brought you into mine. Thanks for growing up with me, and for growing old with me.

ABOUT THE AUTHOR

Melissa Fite Johnson is the author of three full-length collections, most recently *Midlife Abecedarian* (Riot in Your Throat, 2024). Her poems have appeared in *Ploughshares, Pleiades, HAD, Whale Road Review, SWWIM,* and elsewhere. Melissa teaches high school English in Lawrence, KS, where she and her husband live with their dogs.

ABOUT THE PRESS

Riot in Your Throat is an independent press that
publishes fierce, feminist poetry.

Support independent authors, artists, and presses.

Visit us online:
www.riotinyourthroat.com

RIOT IN YOUR THROAT BOOKS

All Possible Histories – Sonia Greenfield
Avoiding the Rapture – Karen J Weyant
Bad Animal – Kathryn Bratt-Pfotenhauer
Borrowing Your Body – Laura Passin
Brilliant Little Body – Brett Elizabeth Jenkins
Dispatches from Frontier Schools – Sarah Beddow
Exquisite Bloody, Beating Heart – Courtney LeBlanc
Green – Melissa Fite Johnson
Little Beast – Sara Quinn Rivara
Somewhere, a Woman Lowers the Hem of Her Skirt – Laurie Rachkus Uttich
Where the Water Begins – Kimberly Casey

www.ingramcontent.com/pod-product-compliance
Lightning Source LLC
Chambersburg PA
CBHW030500130626
46549CB00007B/2798